REAL LIVE SCIENCE

JAY INGRAM

illustrated by
TINA HOLDCROFT

OWL

Greey de Pencier Books

Owl Books are published by Greey de Pencier Books Inc.,
370 King St. West, Suite 300, Toronto, Ontario M5V 1J9

OWL and the Owl character are trademarks of Owl Communications.
Greey de Pencier Books Inc. is a licensed user of trademarks of
Owl Communications.

Distributed in the United States by Firefly Books (U.S.) Inc.,
230 Fifth Avenue, Suite 1607, New York, NY 10001.

The publisher and author wish to thank the Government of Canada's Science Culture
Canada program and the Public Awareness Campaign on Science and Technology
for their generous support of this project.

Canadian Cataloguing in Publication Data

Ingram, Jay
          Real Live Science

Includes index.
ISBN 1-895-688-00-0 (bound) ISBN 0-920775-87-X (pbk.)

1. Scientific recreations - Juvenile literature.
2. Science - Canada - Juvenile literature.
3. Scientists - Canada - Biography - Juvenile
literature. I. Holdcroft, Tina. II. Title.

Q164.I54 1992   j507'.8   C92-093858-2

The experiments in this book have been tested, and are safe when conducted as
instructed. The publisher accepts no responsibility for any damage caused or
sustained due to the use or misuse of ideas or materials featured in the experiments
or activities in *Real Live Science*.

Design and art direction: Julia Naimska
Back cover photo: ©Patrick Nichols

Printed in Hong Kong

B   C   D   E   F   G   H

CONTENTS

INTRODUCTION

This is a book about science, and about scientists. You're going to meet some top-notch scientists and find out how to do experiments at home that are like the experiments they do in their labs and fieldwork. You can try everything from producing a miniature solar system to reading a set of dinosaur footprints.

Science is a bunch of questions, and nobody has all the answers. When you do the activities in this book, you'll feel what it's like to be a scientist, looking for those answers. For starters, here's an experiment that's simple enough to do at home, with a result so mysterious that scientists *still* haven't figured it out! It's one of my favorites.

All you need is a flash camera or a flash attachment that you can set off without putting film in the camera, a towel or two and a completely dark room. A windowless bathroom or a small room in a basement would be perfect. (Most clothes closets would be too small.) Wait until night, then cover any mirrors with a towel and stuff another in the gap below the door. After you've made the room completely black, wait several minutes to allow your eyes to adjust to the dark. The longer you can wait, the better the experiment will be.

1 Bring the flash up beside your ear, aim it at the room in front of you, keep your head and eyes still, and press the flash button. (Don't point the flash into your eyes or at any reflecting surface — you could harm your eyes.) For an instant, you'll see the room in the light from the flash, but the glare will be too great to make out any detail. Now just wait, keeping your head still and your eyes steady. Slowly and mysteriously, a detailed picture of the room will begin to form. You can see everything in it, even things you didn't have time to notice when the flash went off. It's all there in black and white!

2 Wait for a few minutes, until the image has faded away, and try the experiment again. This time move your head after the image has formed. You should find that the picture of the room suddenly disappears.

3 Before you try the experiment a third time, hold your hand up in front of your face. Set off the flash and then quickly drop your hand down to your side. When the after-image forms, you'll have the strange experience of seeing your hand in front of you while you feel it hanging at your side.

The after-image is called "Bidwell's Ghost," after the man who discovered it in 1894, Shelford Bidwell. Even now, a hundred years later, there are still some mysteries about these after-images. We know that there are two kinds of light receptors in the eye — rods and cones — and it's the rods that are sensitive to dim light. By adjusting your eyes to the dark room, you're bringing the rods to their most sensitive. The sudden flash of light overwhelms them, and it takes a few seconds for them to recover and reveal the picture of the room. But no one understands why the picture disappears if you move your eyes from side to side.

That's what this book is all about: explorations you can do yourself, just like the ones that real live scientists do. You'll delve into everything from volcanic lava to snowballs to life in outer space. Have fun!

GET THE PICTURE?

Dr. Steven Zucker,
artificial intelligence specialist

hen Steven Zucker was a kid, his garage was filled with old electronic equipment like walkie-talkies and short-wave radios. He spent hours in that garage, tinkering with the buttons and dials. Today he still works with electronic equipment (not in the garage though), and one of the things he's trying to figure out is why our brains work better than any computer. Our brains are especially good at identifying what our eyes see.

Think of all the bicycles you see every day, and how different each one looks. They come in different sizes and colors. Sometimes you see them in the sunshine, sometimes in shadow. They might be a block away, or right beside you. You can see a bicycle from the side, head-on or at an angle, and still know that it is a bicycle.

Even if you catch just a glimpse of a pair of handlebars, right away your brain fills in the blanks and you say to yourself: "It's a bicycle." But a computer, no matter how sophisticated it is, would not be able to recognize most of those images of bicycles. Steven wants to make computers recognize things with just a few pieces of the picture, the way our brilliant brains can.

What Is It?

Test your brain with this very incomplete picture. Take a good look: do you know what this is? If you're not sure, try squinting or holding the picture farther away or wiggling it back and forth.

This picture of a panda doesn't really look like a panda. It has very little detail for your brain to work with, and the little squares are distracting. But if you blur the squares by squinting your eyes or moving the picture, your brain is able to make its own picture from the dark and light areas. Do you see it?

A computer wouldn't recognize
this animal. Do you?

Familiar Faces

You can turn your own face into a picture like this. You need a good photo of yourself — the bigger the better — a black marker, a pencil and a ruler.

1 Use the enlarging feature on a photocopier to make a large copy of your picture so that the distance from the top of your head to the bottom of your chin is about 12 to 15 cm (5 to 6 in.).

2 With a ruler, draw a grid on the picture, dividing it up carefully into equal little squares. Make about 13 to 15 squares across, and 18 to 20 from top to bottom.

3 Now look at each square and decide whether it's mostly dark, mostly white or in-between. If it's mostly dark, make the whole square completely black with the marker. If it's mostly light, leave it white. If it's in-between, shade the square gray with your pencil.

4 If you want to make your picture even more of a puzzle, trace the grid onto a piece of white paper and shade in the gray and black squares again. You'll get rid of more "clues" that show through from the real photo.

5 Or you can make the picture more lifelike by using different pencils or markers to get more shades. If you have black, dark gray, medium gray, light gray and white your picture will be more recognizable.

Can your friends and family recognize you? Tell them to squint their eyes and look again!

BALANCING ACT

**Dr. Roberta Bondar,
neurologist and astronaut**

Roberta Bondar is Canada's first woman in space. That's not really a big surprise: from the time she was eight she wanted to be a pilot or fly a rocket ship. She even knew the basics of flying a plane before she knew how to drive a car!

As an astronaut, Roberta studies how living in outer space affects our bodies. You've probably seen astronauts in the space shuttle float around their cabin and put their feet on the ceiling. That's because when they're in orbit, their spacecraft is going so fast that it overcomes Earth's pull of gravity, and they become weightless. Remember going over the top on a roller coaster and feeling, just for a second, that you might float away? In a space shuttle, that feeling lasts for days, and it can make life a little tricky.

Weightlessness affects the inner ear. That's the part of your ear deep inside your head that helps you keep your balance. On Earth even with your eyes closed, you still know when your body's not upright because your inner ear tells you so. In space your inner ear doesn't work quite as well.

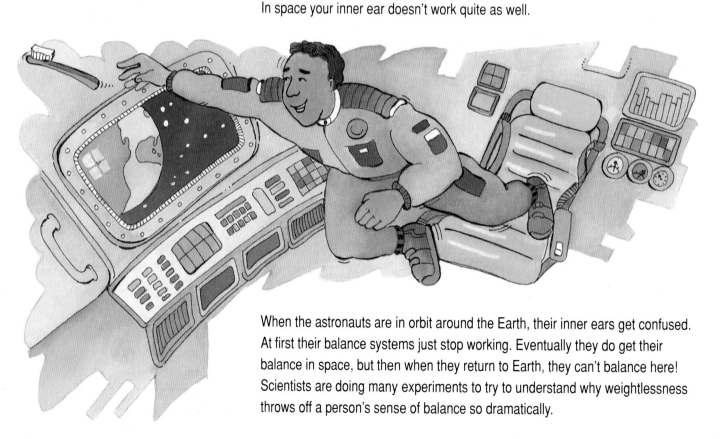

When the astronauts are in orbit around the Earth, their inner ears get confused. At first their balance systems just stop working. Eventually they do get their balance in space, but then when they return to Earth, they can't balance here! Scientists are doing many experiments to try to understand why weightlessness throws off a person's sense of balance so dramatically.

Take a Space Trip at Home

On the space shuttle *Discovery* Roberta Bondar did some experiments to compare how well a person's balance system adapts on Earth to how well it adapts in space. If you have a piano stool or swivel chair, you can try an experiment like the "on Earth" part of Roberta's inner-ear experiment. This version was suggested by Roberta's colleague Doug Watt.

1 Test the chair or stool to be sure it will turn in one direction for a long time without suddenly stopping. Seat a friend in the chair, and blindfold him.

2 Turn the chair steadily in one direction, say clockwise, at a speed of about one complete turn every two or three seconds. Don't let the chair spin by itself and make sure your friend keeps his feet off the floor. At first your friend will feel the turning, but soon he'll get used to the motion and won't feel that he's turning at all.

3 After about 45 seconds or so, stop the chair abruptly. (Be careful your friend doesn't fall off!) He'll feel that he's started to turn in the other direction, even though he's motionless.

How It Works

The inner ear only notices *changes* in movement. When you turned your friend steadily clockwise, his inner ear got used to turning, and soon it figured he wasn't moving at all. Then when the chair stopped turning, his inner ear, figuring he had already been sitting still, incorrectly signalled him that he was turning in the other direction. Your friend's inner ear was confused and not able to do its job properly. But that feeling is nothing compared to the inner-ear confusion astronauts experience in space. Understanding that confusion is one of the things space scientists like Roberta are working on.

DINOSAUR DETECTIVE

Dr. Philip Currie, paleontologist

Phil Currie is a fossil hunter and dinosaur expert in Drumheller, Alberta – right in the heart of dinosaur bone country. Phil knew for a long time that he'd study dinosaurs when he grew up. It all started one day when he opened his box of cereal and a plastic Dimetrodon fell out. Even though Dimetrodon, an extinct reptile, isn't really a dinosaur, it was enough to get him started.

Phil and his colleagues have found some really unusual fossils. They found a nestful of baby Ankylosaurs in the Gobi Desert in China and even a nest of eggs with dinosaur embryos in them in Alberta. The eggs were found in the last ten minutes of a three-week dig!

Sometimes dinosaur detectives like Phil Currie have very few clues to work with. There may not even be any bones to examine, just footprints. But even footprints can tell you a lot about the dinosaurs and how they lived.

For instance, look at this beautifully preserved set of tracks in the rock from Grande Cache, Alberta. There are two types of prints, but they were made by just one animal: an Ankylosaur, a heavily armored, four-footed dinosaur. Those funny marks that look like fossils of crescent rolls were made by the front feet. They are a different shape from the back feet, in the same way that the front paws of bears are different from their back paws.

An Ankylosaur left these footprints 120 million years ago in what is now Grande Cache, Alberta.

Whodunit?

You can be a dinosaur detective too. Study these footprints preserved in the rock and figure out what they mean.

This mess of tracks tells a very exciting and dangerous story. If you can answer the questions about the footprints, you should be able to figure out what happened. (Hint: Try to figure out first what

happens to any animal's footprints -– even yours — when they change from walking to running. How do they look different?)

1 How many dinosaurs were here altogether?

2 The dinosaur walking in from the bottom of the page suddenly began taking larger steps. Can you figure out why?

3 One dinosaur changed direction and left, at the right edge of the scene. Why were his steps longer too?

4 What happened where the footprints come together in the center of the scene?

Take a look at the answers on page 47 to see how you rate as a dinosaur detective.

THE MAGIC OF MEMORY

Allan Paivio became hooked on scientific research when he attended a course on how to be confident in public, give good speeches, and remember people's names. It was the remembering that fascinated him, and today he spends his time trying to understand how our memories work.

Allan is particularly interested in the pictures we see in our minds when we remember something, and how our other senses — hearing, smell, feeling and taste — contribute to those pictures. Maybe you remember a song you heard a lot when you were little, or the special feeling of a favorite stuffed toy. Hearing the song again or touching something fuzzy after a long time can bring memories flooding back into your mind. But even when these other senses bring memories back, they bring them back as pictures. You'll see the uncle who sang you the song or the teddy bear in your old room.

But some things are a lot harder to remember, like shopping lists. You can remember most of the things you need to buy, but you forget *the most important thing!* The problem is that there's nothing about a shopping list that makes it memorable. But if you use Allan's system for linking the items on that list with mental pictures, you'll remember more. Here's how you can prove that to yourself.

Dr. Allan Paivio, psychologist

You Must Remember This

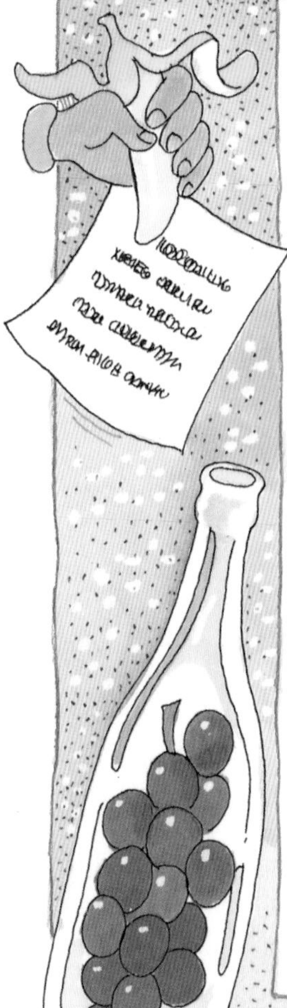

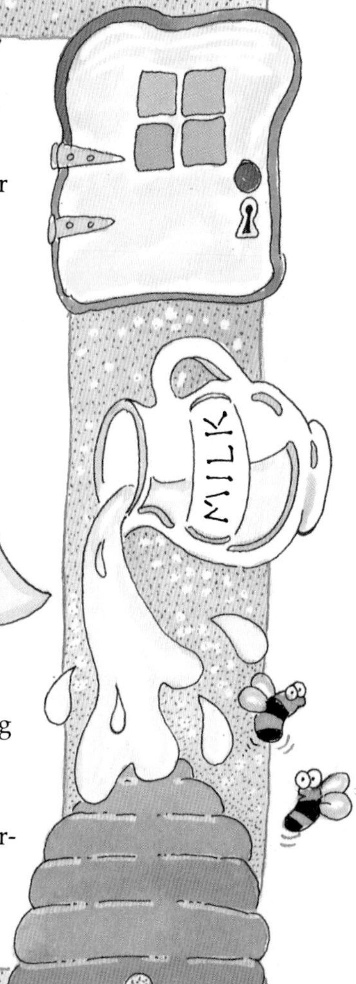

Look at this simple rhyme.

One is a bun, two is a shoe
Three is a tree, four is a door
Five is a hive, six is sticks
Seven is heaven, eight is a gate
Nine is wine, and ten is a pen.

Take a few minutes to memorize the rhyme. It is easy to memorize since the words rhyme with the numbers from one to ten. Make sure you've got them down pat. Whenever you have to remember a list, picture each item on that list together with one item from the rhyme.

Need to buy cheese at the store? Imagine cheese on a bun — that's number one. Want eggs? Imagine them sitting in your shoe — that's number two. It doesn't matter how silly the picture you make is; the important thing is to pair the things you're trying to remember with the poem you know.

Take a look at this list of words:

bed
hand
chair
horse
truck
flower
nose
doll
skirt
dog

Try to memorize the words using the "One is a bun" rhyme. Test yourself in a few hours and see how well you do. You'll never forget how to remember again!

SNOWED UNDER

Dr. Peter Adams, physical geographer

What is the difference between ice and snow? Not as much as you might think. The soft, fluffy stuff can easily be changed into the rock-hard slippery version. They're both just frozen water: the only real difference between them is the amount of air inside. Snow is full of air — it's riddled with little channels and pockets. In ice these little air spaces are cut off from each other and become isolated air bubbles. If you squeeze snow really hard, you begin to close off those little corridors of air, and the snow starts to become ice.

Peter Adams is interested in how snow naturally becomes ice, especially on lakes. Ice forms on a lake when the lake water freezes, but snow that gets packed down on top can become ice too. This is how giant glaciers of the Arctic and the Rocky Mountains form: thousands of years of snowfalls get packed down and change to ice.

Peter says the trick to making good snowballs is to catch the snow at just the right time. With some help from Bill Pruitt (another snow expert), he's come up with tips for…

Perfect Snowballs

1 Check the temperature before you go outside. If it is around freezing, chances are the snow that's falling will already be good snowball snow. Fresh snow at near freezing temperatures is usually filled with snowflakes that have long arms. When these long arms get tangled, the snow becomes sticky and holds together.

2 Be brave: dare to pack cold snow with your bare hands. When you pack a snowball, you're pushing the flakes into each other and tangling them up. But your hands are also melting a little of the snow on the surface of the ball, then letting it freeze again as a thin layer of ice. That ice helps hold the snowball together.

However, if the temperature is way below freezing, it's going to be much harder to melt any of the snow, even with pressure and the warmth of bare hands. Without a coating of ice, the ball is much more likely to fall apart.

3 Avoid snow that's been on the ground for a long time. The longer snow lies around, the worse it is for snowballs, because the long arms of the snowflakes gradually break off and they turn into round hard grains. These are no good for snowballs. They hardly stick to each other at all. That's why they're called "sugar snow."

4 Avoid snow that is too wet. You can't make a good snowball from slush. A little bit of water, as there is in fresh snow, is good because it helps a snowball stick together. But when snow is soaked through and through with water, it won't refreeze.

5 Be a good scientist and keep records. The next time you go outside and find perfect snow-ball-making snow, write down the temperature, how long ago the snow fell, and whether the sun has been shining on the snow you used. Then you'll know exactly what conditions are ideal for making perfect snowballs.

APES ON THE GO

Dr. Biruté Galdikas, anthropologist

As far back as Biruté Galdikas can remember, she always loved orangutans. When she was growing up, she read about these apes in books and watched them at the local zoo. She thinks one of the reasons they appealed to her was their calmness, their slow and unhurried life.

Today Biruté spends part of her time teaching in British Columbia, but her heart is in Indonesia. She runs Camp Leakey in the Indonesian part of the island of Borneo. There she and her researchers follow orangutans day in and day out and study their habits to learn more about these mysterious animals. And she's convinced they do indeed live a blissfully slow and easy life in the treetops.

It's not easy tracking orangutans and recording the details of their lifestyle, even though Biruté has been doing this work for 20 years. You have to follow them as they move. If they're in the trees, they're hard to miss, but once they get on the ground, Biruté says, "they can just vanish!" And chasing orangutans in the Borneo jungle means working in incredible heat and humidity, and having your blood sucked by disease-carrying insects, among other things.

You can do exactly the same sort of research Biruté does, without ever leaving your neighborhood. Track a human the way she tracks an orangutan, and write up your own research report, called a time budget.

Every Minute Counts

1 Choose a subject: your sister, brother, or a parent. Don't choose someone outside your family since you won't be around them enough to study them.

2 List the activities you expect your subject to do, such as eating, playing, watching television, working, reading, talking and sleeping (both napping and at night).

3 Now, watch your subject. Biruté and her team usually follow the same orangutan for ten days, watching it from when it gets out of the nest in the morning to the time it beds down in a new nest at night. If it's not practical for you to follow your subject *that* closely, try to do just a few hours at a time. And for best results, don't let your subject see you watching.

4 As you watch, write down the amount of time your subject spends on each activity. You can add up the minutes later and show your results on a graph.

The scientists watching orangutans at Camp Leakey record their research on a graph something like the one you see here.

See how your human subject's daily activities compare with a typical orangutan's. This graph shows roughly how a young orangutan, about the age of an 8- to 12-year-old human, spends its day.

After 12 hours of sleep, it's up at dawn, 6:00 a.m. or so. Until sundown, 12 hours later, there will be about 2 1/2 hours of moving through the jungle (mostly looking for food), another 2 1/2 hours of resting with some play and about 7 hours of snacking!

You probably won't find any of your subjects spending 7 hours eating. But you might be surprised to find out just how humans do spend their time.

DON'T BUG ME

Dr. Roger Downer, entomologist

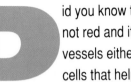id you know that insects have blood? It's not red and it doesn't flow through blood vessels either, but, like ours, it is full of cells that help protect the insects from diseases. Studying these cells is Roger Downer's latest insect project. He's also studied their nervous systems, their muscles and their fat. (Yes, even insects have fat!)

Although most of us don't notice insects — unless they're buzzing around our ears — Roger finds them just as complex and interesting as other animals. You just have to take the time to look at them closely.

Since Roger knows a lot about insects, he has some ideas about how you can make an insect repellent that works. But to keep insect pests such as mosquitoes away from you, we need to know something about how these pests find you. Scientists know that our body heat, moisture and even the colors we wear can attract mosquitoes to us. (They seem to like dark colors better than light ones.) These insects also depend on their sense of smell, although we're not quite sure what they can pick up. They can detect a chemical called lactic acid in our perspiration, and probably a lot of other things too. But a mosquito's favorite smells are likely very different from yours — maybe they like the smell of chocolate chip cookies, maybe they don't. So to find out what turns them off, you'll have to experiment with different ingredients for your repellent.

The Sweet Smell of Success

1 To begin, you'll need to round up a few items from the fridge or the kitchen cupboards: chopped onions, lemon juice, cloves or other spices. Maybe mosquitoes can smell things we can't: try cornstarch or sugar too.

2 Outdoor plants are possibilities as well. Pick some leaves, flowers or roots, but stick to the garden when you're picking. Avoid any wild plant you don't know, or you could end up with a poison ivy rash instead of mosquito bites. Organic gardeners have found that garlic plants repel some insects, and Roger thinks the chopped bulbs might work against mosquitoes too.

3 Mash up each of your ingredients separately with a little water or vegetable oil to make a liquid repellent. You will be able to test only one or two of your repellents at a time.

4 Before you go outside, smear one arm with a test repellent and, if you dare, leave the other arm untouched. You can judge how well the repellent works by counting the mosquito bites on each arm. Or try another of your repellents on the other arm and compare the bite counts.

5 Try a store-bought repellent on one arm and your best repellent on the other. What if you get the same number of bites on both arms? Then perhaps you've really discovered something!

By the way, don't forget to wash up when the experiment is over. You might be quite smelly, and you're supposed to be driving away mosquitoes, not your family, friends and pets.

TAKE YOUR CHANCES

Dr. Paul Corey, biostatistician

What's the difference between Snakes and Ladders and chess? In chess you get to choose your moves, but Snakes and Ladders is a game of chance: the dice control your marker, you don't. As a kid, Paul Corey became fascinated by puzzles, especially puzzles that seem like games of chance but turn out to have hidden factors in control.

Paul's job at the University of Toronto is to understand what role chance plays in disease. Remember the last time the flu was around? Some kids in your class got it, some didn't. Why? Part of the reason is chance. But often what looks like chance can be explained scientifically. Those are the explanations Paul looks for.

Imagine you are on a big TV game show. You have to guess which of the three doors has the fabulous prize behind it. Let's say you pick the door on the right. The host of the show then says: "Okay, I've looked behind the door on the *left*, and the prize isn't there. Do you want to change your mind, or stick with the door on the right?" You panic for a second. But you could still be right. Why bother changing? Paul suggests you can find out what you should do by trying this experiment with your friends.

Step Right Up, Folks

You need two friends, three cups and a small object you can hide under one of the cups, like an eraser or a peanut. One friend will be the "Sticker" and the other will be the "Changer." Set up a very long record sheet to keep score.

Sticker   Changer   Nobody

1 While your friends aren't looking, put the object under one of the cups. Ask your friends to decide between them where it is. Once they have chosen, point to one of the other two cups, one you know is not hiding the object, and tell them: "It's not under this cup."

2 The Sticker has to stick to the original choice, but the Changer has to switch. Now reveal the object and make a record of who was right: the Sticker, the Changer or neither one.

3 For good results you should try this 100 times. If you don't have that much time, do it as many times as you can. Then count up the scores and see who did the best. Are you surprised?

Like many card tricks, this game makes the players think they have the same chances of winning. After all, neither the Sticker nor the Changer is told where the object is. But the Changer's the lucky one: she gets extra information about where the object isn't!

How It Works

The Sticker will be right one third of the time on his first guess, by chance. Since the first guess is all he gets, he will get about 33 out of 100 right.

But it's different for the Changer. One third of the time, the object will be under the cup she chose first, and you are making her guess wrong by forcing her to switch. But the other two thirds of the time, the object won't be where she thought it was; it will be under one of the other two cups. When you tell her which of those two it is not under, you force her to switch to the right cup — and that will happen about 67 times out of 100!

Surprising as it seems, it's better to be a Changer in this game. In fact, it's so surprising that when this puzzle appeared in a newspaper, some mathematicians wrote in to say the answer was wrong!

21

TASTE IS TRICKY

Dr. Linda Malcolmson, food scientist

Do you like chocolate? How about Brussels sprouts? Linda Malcolmson is interested in why we like the foods we do. She knows that taste is only one of many reasons why some foods are our favorites, and it may not even be the most important reason. In her research, Linda is trying to find out more about the other reasons. She says if we had only our sense of taste, eating wouldn't be nearly as interesting as it is!

Our tongues can detect only four tastes: sweet, sour, salty and bitter. Much of what we think of as taste is actually odor. Remember the last time you had a bad cold, and everything tasted the same? That's because your nose was out of order. Color and texture are also important features. Most people love foods that are crunchy, but absolutely *hate* anything that's slimy. Linda herself wouldn't eat raisins when she was a kid because she didn't like their unusual texture.

It's not just the foods themselves that make up our minds. Our expectations about foods also play a very important role. We can easily be fooled by foods that are not what they seem. Try fooling your friends with these experiments Linda has suggested.

Come to Your Senses

Mix 8 mL (1½ tsp.) of cinnamon with 25 mL (5 tsp.) of sugar. Ask a few friends to close their eyes and hold their noses, then put some of the mixture on their tongues. If you ask them what it is, they'll all say "sugar." When they unplug their noses (but keep their eyes closed), ask again. Suddenly they'll know the cinnamon is there.

Put some peanut butter, cheese, ketchup and other everyday foods in separate cups covered with thin cloth or tissue. Ask your friends to close their eyes and try to identify each food by sniffing. When all we have to go on is our sense of smell, we're not nearly so sure what food is in front of us.

For this experiment you need some packages of light-colored jelly dessert and some dark food coloring, such as green, red and blue. Prepare the gelatin as usual, with the help of an adult, but when you add the boiling water, also add enough food coloring to change the color. Try these combinations:

- lemon jelly with green food coloring
- lemon jelly with purple food coloring (blue and red mixed)
- peach jelly with red coloring

When you ask your friends what flavor each jelly is, they'll probably say the green one is lime, the purple one is grape and the red one is cherry. You can't believe everything you see!

A TALE OF A TREE

Dr. Alan Mitchell, forest scientist

You probably know you can tell the age of a tree by counting its rings. But do you know that the rings reveal much more than that? Al Mitchell is a forester who studies the growth of Douglas fir trees. These trees usually live for 300 to 500 years. Some get to be over a thousand years old! The rings of a tree this age can tell a tree historian like Al plenty.

Every year a tree adds a layer of new wood around the outside, just inside the bark – so every year the tree gets thicker as well as taller. Each new layer leaves a ring that you can see in the stump when the tree is cut down. If you know what year the tree was cut down, you can work your way in from the outside edge and identify each year that the tree was alive.

A middle-aged Douglas fir in Washington's Mt. Rainier National Park

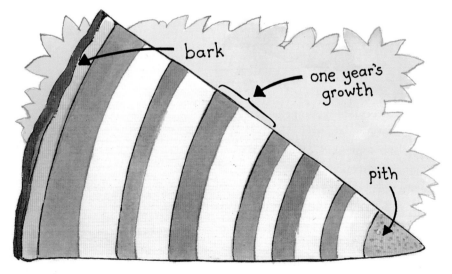

Each ring has two parts, one light and one dark. The light part is "springwood," made when the tree is growing quickly in the spring. The dark part of the ring is "summerwood." You can tell from the width of the springwood or summerwood how good the conditions for growth were during that season. (There's no "fallwood" or "winterwood" because trees don't grow in those seasons.)

Timber-r-r-r!

Here's the stump of a tree that was cut down in the fall of 1992. Read the history of this tree in its rings and see whether they can tell you the answers to these questions. Check the answers on page 47 to see how well you did.

1 Local farmers tell you that there were swarms of insects here for three or four years in the 1980s. The insects ate so many leaves that most trees just couldn't grow at all during those summers. Is there any evidence of that in the stump?

2 In 1981 the valley had a cool, unpleasant spring followed by a hot, wet summer that was perfect for growing trees. Does your stump tell you if there were other years like that? Which years?

3 Your records show that a forest fire swept through the valley in 1986, but you need to find out if it got as far as this tree before the rains put it out. Did it?

4 A logger in town says he hammered a long nail as far as he could into this tree when it was at least ten years old. You've been lucky enough to find a nail embedded in the stump. Was the logger right about the tree's age?

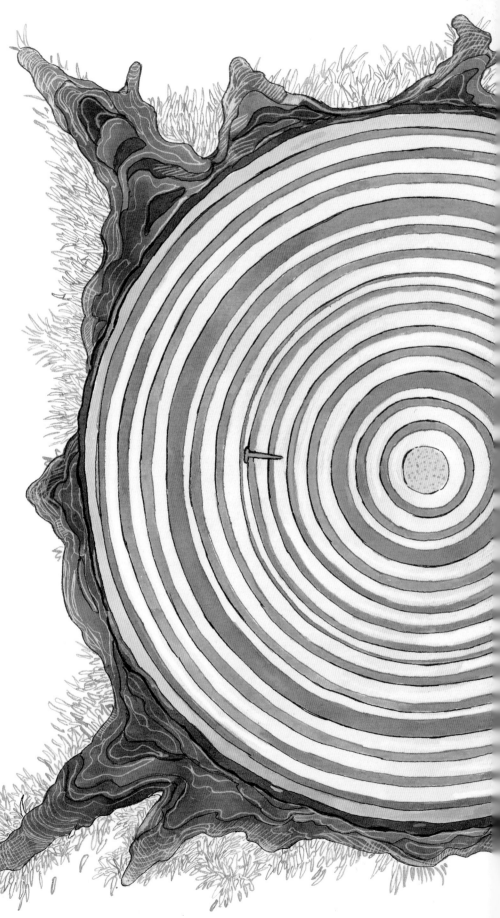

LIFE IN THE ARCTIC

**Dr. Harold (Buster) Welch,
marine biologist**

Buster Welch got an early start as a biologist. By the time he was seven years old, he was already tying the artificial flies used in fly fishing and selling them. He made enough money to buy a baritone horn and an outboard motor. But more important, he was already hooked on fish. Now Buster studies how fish and many other forms of life survive and even thrive in the Arctic.

Animals that live under or near the Arctic ice have one big problem that people don't have to worry about: salt.

People can't drink salt water when they're thirsty, because their bodies have to expel a lot of fluid to wash out the salt. If they drank it, they'd end up even thirstier because they would lose more water than they'd taken in.

But animals that live near or in the salty Arctic Ocean have no fresh water nearby. So they have found ways around the salt water problem. They get the water they need from the food they eat, and they avoid taking in salt water. Seals can swallow food while they're under water without gulping down seawater at the same time. Sea birds drink some seawater, but they have their own trick: they weep salty tears. Their special tears get rid of a lot of salt without losing too much water, so the birds won't get thirsty again.

What would *you* drink if you were stranded on an Arctic island? Understanding what happens to salt water when it turns to ice could help save your life. Try Buster's water trick in the safety of your own kitchen.

The Arctic Survival Trick

1 Rinse out an empty, clear plastic 2-L (2-qt.) pop bottle. Carefully cut the top off at the shoulder with a knife or a pair of scissors.

2 Fill the bottle with water, to about 3 cm (1 in.) from the top. Dissolve 75 mL (5 tbsp.) of salt in the water. This mixture is about as salty as real seawater. Taste it. Now put the bottle in the freezer, or outside if it's below freezing.

3 Wait for the top third of the water to freeze. (It will take quite a while.) The part that's frozen solid will look whitish. Lick a bit of the ice. How salty is it, compared with the liquid salt water?

4 Stand the bottle in a bowl filled with hot water from the tap. Leave the bottle there for two hours, or until all but the top

2 cm (3/4 in.) of ice has melted. Stick your tongue onto the ice — how salty is it now?

5 Lift the ice out of the bottle and stand it on its edge in a bowl. Wait a minute or so, until some of the water runs out of the ice, then bite a little piece of the ice at the top. How salty is it now?

You should have found that the ice was getting less and less salty. Why? There's little room between the ice crystals for salt, so when the ice forms, most of the salt stays in the water. And as the ice begins to melt, the small amount of salt trapped inside it falls out. The ice that is left is almost salt-free, and you could melt it to drink. Remember that if you are ever stranded in the Arctic!

FEET ARE NEAT

Dr. Michael Hawes, kinesiologist

Did you know that in your lifetime your feet will hit the ground about 10 million times? And if you think that your feet are just simple platforms for walking on, consider this: you have 26 bones, 114 ligaments (the stretchy bands that connect the bones) and 20 muscles in *each* of your feet.

Feet are very complex because they have so many functions. As you walk, your feet have to take the shock of landing on the ground with your weight on top of them; then they have to push that weight up into the air again. And while they're doing that, your feet keep you from tipping over sideways or falling forwards or backwards.

When Michael Hawes was in school, he liked sports a lot more than science class. Now that he's director of a sport anthropology lab, he's found a way to stay close to sports and be a scientist at the same time. He studies feet, and he's particularly interested in how they fit into shoes, especially sports shoes. He can help you learn things about your feet from your shoes and your footprints.

Follow Those Footprints

One of the most important parts of your foot is the arch. It is shaped like an archery bow: the foot bones are curved, and there's a ligament that joins them like the bowstring. When your foot hits the ground, especially when you're running, the arch flattens, then bounces back. That bounce-back gives your foot energy to help get it off the ground for the next step. Researchers have shown that even springy sports shoes aren't as bouncy as the arch in your foot.

ligament

average arch

high arch

low arch

Sole Searching

Some people have high arches, like a very tightly strung bow, while others have low arches, like a loose bow. Look at the bottoms of the oldest pair of sneakers you own. See where the heels are worn away? People with high arches usually wear away the outside of the heel, while people with lower arches wear their sneakers away along the inside of the heel.

Powder Prints

You can get a more detailed picture of your feet and arches by making powder prints. Sprinkle talcum powder on the soles of your bare feet, then step onto colored paper or a velour towel.

Compare the print of your foot with these drawings. If the front of your foot is almost completely separated from the back, you've got a high arch. If you can see the print of the entire bottom of your foot, you've got a low arch or "flat feet." Being flatfooted was once thought to be unhealthy, but doctors now believe it's no problem at all. So what kind of arches do you have?

THE SCIENCE OF SLEEP

Dr. Janet Mullington, neuroscientist

t's funny, isn't it? Although you spend only about two hours a day eating, and as much as nine hours sleeping, you probably know a lot more about your eating habits than you do about your sleeping habits. Do you know how many hours you sleep? Or when is the best time to go to bed?

For scientists like Janet Mullington, sleep is full of mysteries. If you live to be 80 years old, you'll have spent about 25 years sound asleep – but we don't know why. What goes on in our brains while we're sleeping? Why do we sometimes feel we haven't slept very well even though we slept as many hours as usual?

We've all heard of "insomniacs" (people who have trouble sleeping). But there are also people who have trouble staying awake. These are the people Janet is studying. They have a disorder called "narcolepsy": they can fall asleep at any time, even when they're eating or listening to someone talk. Janet is hoping that by keeping detailed records of their sleep, she can help her patients to organize their sleep better. If they rest at scheduled times, they might not have as many "sleep attacks."

Keep a "sleep log" to figure out how much sleep you need and when you need it. Janet has created a special version of her lab's sleep log for you to try.

Sleep Like a Log

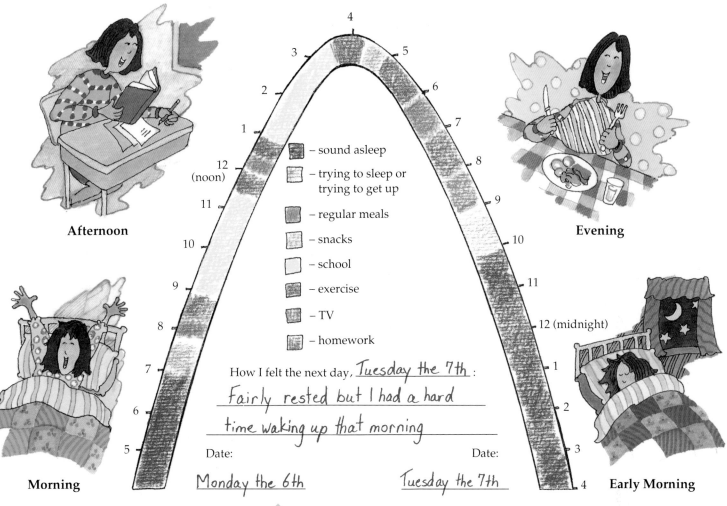

- sound asleep
- trying to sleep or trying to get up
- regular meals
- snacks
- school
- exercise
- TV
- homework

Afternoon

Evening

Morning

Early Morning

How I felt the next day, _Tuesday the 7th_ :
Fairly rested but I had a hard time waking up that morning

Date: _Monday the 6th_   Date: _Tuesday the 7th_

Lots of things could affect your sleep. This log will let you keep track of some of them: naps, meals and snacks, and how you spend your after-school and evening time.

1 Copy the sleep chart you see here (just the black lines). Make one chart for each day over a two-week period, so that you can cover two weekends. Staple the charts together.

2 Start your log on a Monday morning. Write in the date. Use the colors shown to chart how long you slept and the time it took you to get out of bed.

3 As the day goes on, use the other colors to fill in naps, meals, snacks and activities.

4 At bedtime, mark the time you got into bed. _Don't_ watch the clock until you fall asleep, or you'll have a hard time drifting off! Just take a guess the next morning at how long it took you to get to sleep.

5 On Tuesday morning, start your next chart. At the end of the day, go back to Monday's chart and note whether you felt rested on Tuesday. That's how you can tell whether Monday's pattern

of activity led to a good night's sleep that night.

When you have filled out all 14 charts this way, you might be able to see some important patterns. You might find, for example, that you can get up more quickly if you skip your late-night snack. Or maybe you can fall asleep more easily on Sunday night if you have your homework done. If you've been searching for the key to better sleep, it's a dream come true!

TOILET PAPER ASTRONOMY

Dr. James Hesser, astrophysicist

A globular star cluster thousands of light-years from Earth

magine jumping on a beam of light and traveling through space. Twelve months from now, you would have traveled 9,460,000,000,000 km (6 million million mi.) across the universe — that's one light-year, the distance that light can travel in a year. In four years and four months, you would have just enough time to fly the 40,680,000,000,000 km (25,425,000,000,000 mi.) from the Earth to Alpha Centauri, the nearest star beyond our Sun, at a speed of 300,000 km (186,000 mi.) per second!

Jim Hesser (kids call him "Hesser the Professor") studies globular clusters, huge swarms of hundreds of thousands of stars, like the one you see here. If one of these clusters were as close to Earth as Alpha Centauri is, Hesser the Professor says it would look unlike anything we've ever seen: "The sky would be ablaze with light! There would be stars everywhere you looked, stars of different brightness and in every color of the rainbow."

But we'll never see this sight, because these clusters of stars are three to four *thousand* light-years away, a thousand times farther than Alpha Centauri. So Hesser the Professor has a long way to look before he finds his clusters. He knows just how hard it is to understand the immense distances of space, but he can show you how a lowly roll of toilet paper can help you to imagine them.

Roll Out the Solar System

All you need for this trip to the planets is a roll of toilet paper, ten friends and an area that's long, straight and flat. If it's dry with no wind outside, you could do it on a sidewalk or a playground. If not, you'll need a hallway that's at least 33 m (110 ft.) long; a school hall-way or gym would be perfect.

The first person — the Sun — takes the roll of toilet paper and holds the first sheet down, without tear-ing it off. Now roll the toilet paper out in a straight line. (The planets are almost never lined up as per-fectly as this, though.) Mercury, the first planet, stands on the third sheet, Venus takes the fifth sheet and so on. This chart shows the distances to all the planets.

Planet	Sheet	Millions of Kilometres (Miles)	
Sun	0	0	
Mercury	3	58	(36)
Venus	5	108	(68)
Earth	7.5	130	(94)
Mars	11.5	228	(142)
Jupiter	39	778	(485)
Saturn	72	1 427	(892)
Uranus	144	2870	(1794)
Neptune	225	4497	(2811)
* Pluto	300	6000	(3488)

* This is an average distance to Pluto. Until 1999 it will be a little closer in than Neptune, but then will again become the most distant planet, all the way out at sheet 367.

From Earth's position you can barely see those last few planets as you look down the line. But to astronomers, measuring our solar system is like measuring the distance to the back porch. The planets around the Sun are not very far away at all, compared with the stars of the night sky.

Pluto, at the end of the roll, is only $5\frac{1}{2}$ light-*hours* away. To roll out the toilet-paper equivalent to Alpha Centauri, more than four light-*years* away, you'd need more than 7,000 rolls! And to reach Hesser the Professor's star clusters, a thousand times farther away? You'd have to have enough toilet paper to circle the Earth.

ANCIENT GARBAGE

Brian Kooyman loves garbage, the older the better. In fact, he *studies* garbage: he's an archeologist. Archeologists sometimes dig up ancient Egyptian tombs, and they might even stumble across a mysterious carved head in the Mexican jungle. But most of the time the picture they paint of our distant past comes from used tools, broken pots and the scraps our ancestors threw out after dinner. In other words, garbage.

Brian has been digging up and examining some very unusual garbage. For nearly 6,000 years, at a special place in southern Alberta, hunters killed thousands of buffalo by driving them over a cliff. At the bottom the hunters processed the buffalo meat. The name of the cliff in Blackfoot is *Estipah-sikikini-kots*. The English translation is Head-Smashed-In Buffalo Jump (in memory of a young boy who was crushed under a herd of buffalo).

Talk about garbage! There's thousands of years worth at Head-Smashed-In, mostly old buffalo bones and discarded carving tools. But what a story they can tell if you know how to read it. Brian says there's no magic to it. "It's detective work, that's all. You learn to look at things in a different way."

Here's your chance to do the work of an archeologist without even leaving your home.

Dr. Brian Kooyman, archeologist

These tools were found at Head-Smashed-In Buffalo Jump. The small arrow head is up to 1,750 years old, but the larger one could be 3,300 years old. In the center is the broken head of a hammer-like tool. On the right is a stone knife used to cut meat.

Archeology at Home

Imagine you're an archeologist 2,000 years from now, and you've just stumbled upon a perfectly preserved room from a house built in the 1990s. Can you identify the objects (or "artifacts," as archeologists call them) found in the room, and figure out what this room was used for?

1 A hollow, flat-bottomed object about the size of a brick. It is made of cloth, rubber and plastic, and the bottom is filled with pockets of air.

2 A ceramic disc with pieces of a baked starchy substance and remnants of a circular chunk of burnt protein, covered with traces of an unidentified red liquid.

3 A large sheet of compressed wood fibers covered on one side with the image of a human with very long hair and pieces of metal all over his — or her? — clothing. The human is standing, holding a stick-like object that has wires running along its length.

4 A large wooden platform the top of which is covered by a soft plastic envelope filled with liquid made up of ancient hydrogen and oxygen molecules. On top of this is a smaller envelope made of natural fibers, filled with a soft, dry substance of chemical composition.

5 A hard plastic object with buttons on it. The numbers and letters on the 12 main buttons suggest a code. The artifact shows evidence of heavy use.

Do these objects sound familiar? Look on page 47 to find out how good you are at archeological detective work.

EYE SPY

**Dr. Jacob Sivak,
physiological opticist**

J acob Sivak has worn thick glasses since he was six years old. He thinks that visiting so many eye doctors made him want to learn more about seeing. Jacob has been studying unusual vision for years. Right now he's trying to figure out how some animals, unlike human beings, manage to see well both under the water and in the air.

When you read these words, the light rays coming from the page travel to your eye. These rays bend when they hit your cornea (the front surface of your eye). Then they are bent some more by the lens inside your eye. The cornea and the lens together bend the rays enough so that they all meet at the very back of your eye (the retina) and form a little picture of the page. That's how you see.

Why do the light rays bend? There are two reasons. First, the surface of your eye is curved rather than flat; second, your eye is watery. Light rays always bend when they move from air to water, or from water to air.

When you are under water, things are a little different. There the light rays are already travelling through water, so when they hit the watery cornea of your eye, they don't bend as much as they should, and everything looks blurry. That's not too much of a problem for us because we don't spend much time in the water, but what about the animals and birds that do?

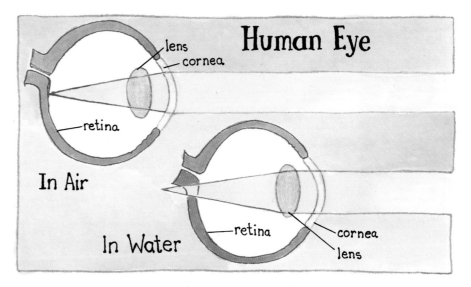

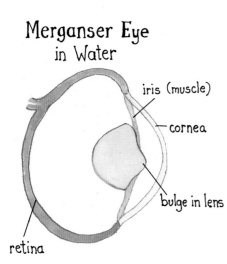

Merganser Eye
in Water

The hooded merganser is a duck-like bird that dives for fish. It has to be able to see clearly under water, or it won't catch any dinner. When the merganser is under water, light rays pass through its corneas with only a little bending, just as they do when passing through human corneas. But the merganser has powerful muscles in each eye to squeeze its lenses. Each lens bulges out so much that it can focus the light rays and allow the merganser to see the fish it's chasing.

Seeing Under the Sea

To see how being under water affects human vision, try this.

You need swimming goggles, a plastic 30-cm (12-in.) ruler, a black crayon or waterproof felt pen and a piece of white plastic that the crayon or pen will write on. If you can't find plastic that you can write on, use a piece of cardboard and wrap it tightly in plastic wrap.

1 Write a message to yourself in letters that are big enough to read when you hold the message 30 cm (12 in.) away from your eyes. If you wear glasses or contact lenses, write a message that you can read without them.

2 Take the ruler, your message and the goggles to the bathtub or a swimming pool. Put your message under water, holding it at the end of the ruler. Now close your eyes, hold your breath, and put your face under water too, with your eyes at the near end of the ruler. Open your eyes. Can you read what you've written? Try moving the message closer, then farther. What happens?

3 Now try reading at the same distances, but with the goggles on. See the difference? Your eyes can't focus light that's travelling from the water in the tub to the water in your corneas, so you see fuzzy letters. But when you put the goggles on, the light travels from water to air to water. That's what your eyes are used to, and so you can see perfectly well.

GOOD VIBRATIONS

Dr. Mary Anne White, chemist

Chemists like Mary Anne White know that the world we live in isn't as simple as it looks. Take heat, for instance: to most of us it seems to flow in a smooth stream, like the warmth of an electric blanket or hot water from a kettle. But for chemists, heat has a jazzier image. They see it as the twitching and shaking of vibrating molecules.

An ice cube is another example of how looks can fool us. Ice seems completely solid, but if you could see inside the tiny ice crystals that make up the cube, you'd be astonished! Most of that rock-hard ice is actually empty space. There are millions of molecules of water in the ice cube, locked frozen together in regular repeating patterns, but between these molecules, there's empty space, like the space between the steel beams of a skyscraper.

What happens if you heat up that ice cube? The water molecules start to vibrate more and more, until some of them snap out of place and the crystals begin to fall apart. The ice cube is melting.

Mary Anne loved the beauty of crystals when she was a kid, and today she works with many exotic materials, trying to figure out how heat flows through them. How do *their* molecules behave? Even with all of today's sophisticated scientific knowledge, there are still some real mysteries about heat.

A close-up look at ice crystals

Hot Ice

Mary Anne has suggested an experiment you can do that scientists have been trying for the last 150 years. If you leave two ice cubes touching each other, they'll eventually stick together. It happens every time, but no one's sure why! Try putting your two ice cubes together in these different ways. See how long it takes them to stick together, and how difficult it is to break them apart.

1 Put one cube on top of another on the kitchen counter. (Side by side they might slide apart.) Watch these carefully, because it won't take long for them to melt completely!

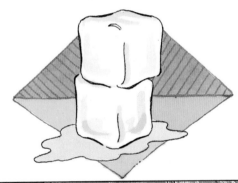

2 Put another pair of cubes in a glass of cold water (the glass must be small enough for the ice cubes to be touching). In this case you know that they're wet. Do they stick faster?

3 Put one ice cube on top of another in the freezer. Do these take much longer to stick than the others? Pile up another pair in the freezer with a few drops of water between them.

Scientists know that for ice cubes to stick together, some water molecules from one cube have to move enough to attach to some water molecules of the other cube. They usually move only if the ice melts, but your cubes will stick together even if they're in the freezer. How can the ice be melting, even a little?

How It Works

Mary Anne thinks the ice cubes in the glass of water might stick together in as little as half an hour, while the pair in the freezer could take days. She suspects that even if the cubes aren't melting much, there are probably just enough water molecules moving around on the surface to make the cubes stick together — but only after a long time.

Try some of your own variations on the experiment. After all, no one's really sure yet why they stick together!

FLIP, FLOP AND FLY

Dr. James DeLaurier, aeronautical engineer, with the Ornithopter

People have spun propellers, burned jet fuel, even inflated balloons and blimps — all to be able to fly. But until September 4, 1991, no one had ever built an engine-powered machine that flaps its wings and flies like a bird. On that day James DeLaurier and his team took a machine they call the Ornithopter (meaning "bird-wing") out to a hill near Toronto, started its engine, and watched it flap its wings and take off.

It all started when James was a schoolkid. It was the first day of a new month, and he tore the old sheet off a small calendar and threw it towards the wastebasket. It didn't just fall in; it glided through the air, flipping over and over. That started James thinking about flight. By the time he was 8, he had already decided to build airplanes when he grew up. Until then, he settled for building and flying model airplanes in special competitions.

Everything that flies, from a mosquito to a jumbo jet, starts by using energy to create motion. Airplanes use engines and birds use their muscles to generate forward motion. As their wings push through the air, the air is forced to change direction. Some of the air is pushed up over the top of each wing, creating suction that pulls the wing up, and some air turns upwards and lifts the wing from underneath.

The combination of suction on top of the wing and pressure from underneath is called "lift force." Test it out on this simple flier suggested by James.

Spread Your Wings

Cut out a rectangle of light cardboard or bristol board, about 20 cm (8 in.) long by 6 cm (2 1/4 in.) wide. wide. Hold the cardboard in the middle of a long side, then give it a little downward push as you let go.

You'll notice your flier doesn't just fall straight down: it ends up some distance away. The push you give it creates forward motion, and the motion generates lift force that makes it fly.

But unlike a bird or an airplane, your flier flips, like the calendar page that James dropped years ago. That's because lift force is strongest at the front edge of a wing. Your flier is so light that the lift force under its front edge can actually flip it over. Then the other edge is at the front, and the flier flips again — and it keeps rotating, like a pinwheel, until finally it hits the ground.

Try these changes to keep your flying machine in the air longer.

1 To make your flier stiffer and stronger, make two creases along the long sides of the flier; then bend one edge up and the other down. Hold it by the edge that bends up, then give it a little downward push. The bent-down edge at the front will help your flier trap more lift force, making it rotate more quickly.

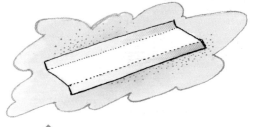

2 The less the flier wobbles around in the air, the farther it can glide between flips. Try adding some stabilizers.

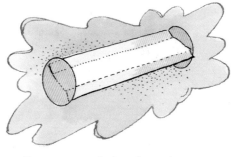

Cut out two circles about 6 cm (2 1/4 in.) in diameter from the same cardboard and glue or tape them to the ends of the wings as shown. They will make your flier steadier. Also, like the bent-down edge, they will catch the wind under the flier's wings and let it be lifted farther.

Now that you know how to harness lift force, you might build your own super flier one day!

VOLCANOES IN THE KITCHEN

Dr. Nancy Van Wagoner, geologist

Dr. Catherine Hickson, geologist

Mount St. Helen's before and after the 1980 eruption

Cathie Hickson still has a rock she collected from beside a campfire when she was six years old. When Nancy Van Wagoner was young, she hiked up a volcano to see what it looked like at the top. Today they both study rocks and volcanoes, and there are still lots of questions they haven't answered yet.

There is a layer of rock inside the Earth (like a thin layer of icing in a cake) that has melted into a red-hot liquid called magma. It's being squeezed by the weight of the land and water above it. But if it finds a weak spot, it "erupts" — it bursts right through in a volcanic eruption. The magma that pours out is called lava.

Cathie was right there when Mount St. Helen's erupted violently in Washington State in 1980. Volcanoes like that one literally blow their tops. Pieces of rock from Mount St. Helen's were found 14 km (9 mi.) away! Others, like the volcanoes on Hawaii and Iceland (and some of the ancient Canadian volcanoes Nancy has discovered), ooze rather than explode. The lava that erupts from them flows as fast as water.

Why do volcanoes erupt in different ways? The secret is in the thickness of the lava. Nancy suggests you make "lava" in your own home using her formula, and you'll see why.

Lava Pancakes

1 Mix the dry ingredients (except the chocolate chips) together. Add the wet ingredients and stir. Don't worry if your lava is a bit lumpy. Molten rock from deep in the Earth is lumpy too.

INGREDIENTS
- 500 mL (2 cups) flour
- 60 mL (4 tbsp.) double-acting baking powder
- 60 mL (4 tbsp.) sugar
- 5 mL (1 tsp.) salt
- 2 eggs, beaten
- 500 mL (2 cups) 2% milk
- 60 mL (4 tbsp.) cooking oil
- 250 g (1 cup) very small chocolate chips
- oil for frying

2 Immediately test the thickness of this lava. Put a few spoonfuls into a cup, stick a straw into it, and slowly blow some bubbles. The bubbles come up through the liquid easily and burst at the surface. This is like free-flowing Hawaiian lava.

3 Let the lava sit for 10 minutes. Inside, the wet baking powder is forming bubbles, just as the gases inside real lava produce bubbles as it cools. Again blow through the straw into the lava in the cup. The bubbles you blow won't move nearly as easily as they did before, because the baking-powder bubbles have thickened the lava. It is now more like the lava from an explosive volcano.

4 Stir the lava to get rid of the bubbles, and add the chocolate chips. These chips are like the crystals you can find in volcanic lava. Crystals make it even harder for the lava to flow. You can see the increased thickness by using the cup and straw once more — but watch out! The harder you blow on this crystalline, bubbly lava, the more likely it is to explode — just like the real stuff.

5 Now for the best part. Heat up a thin layer of oil in a frying pan and drop in blobs of your lava. When the tops are bubbly, flip your lava pancakes and cook them for about 1 minute longer. Then add butter and maple syrup, and eat them up.

WHAT A PAIN

Dr. Ronald Melzack, psychologist

Some people are born without the ability to feel pain. They have a miserable life: they're constantly suffering bad burns because they lean up against a hot stove and don't know it, or they sprain an ankle and make the injury much worse by walking on it. Even though we don't like pain, it helps us. Pain is the body's way of warning us that something is going wrong.

As a child, Ronald Melzack had relatives who were very sick and suffering a lot of pain. Now he's trying to figure out how pain works, and what can be done to help those who have the most serious and long-lasting pain.

Pain takes many forms: it can be "throbbing," "stabbing" or "aching." Then there's "phantom" pain, which usually appears after someone has a foot, a hand, or a whole leg or arm amputated. After the operation, patients may feel excruciating pain coming from the part of their body *that they no longer have!*

Soldiers are often carried off battlefields with terrible wounds and offered powerful pain-killers. But sometimes they refuse the drugs, because the sense of relief they feel from being out of danger is stronger than their pain.

These stories suggest that pain is in your mind as much as it is in the cut or burn that's hurting. Ronald has suggested this experiment to help you see the mind-body connection for yourself.

Use Your Brain to Stop the Pain

1 Fill a large bowl halfway with water, add some ice cubes, and wait a few minutes until the water is ice-cold.

2 Watching the clock, put your hand in the bowl of ice water and leave it there until it hurts so much you can't stand the pain any more. Then take your hand out and make a note of how long you lasted.

3 When you've warmed up, put your hand back in the ice water, but with someone else watching the clock for you. While your hand is in the ice water, think of the absolutely best time you've had in the last few months. It could be anything you've enjoyed: a ball game, a party, anything at all. Concentrate on it, and try to remember every little detail. Now how long can you stand the cold?

4 Try this with your friends, too, without telling them why you're doing it. (It's closer to a true scientific experiment when the subjects don't know what the experiment is all about.)

5 Here's another version of the same experiment that you can do with friends. Don't watch the clock this time. When you can't stand the ache of the cold water any longer, take your hand out and ask a friend to rub the hand that *wasn't* in the water.

You'll probably find that you and your friends can last longer in the ice water when you're thinking about something more pleasant. And you may find that rubbing the hand that isn't hurting will sometimes take away the pain from the icy hand.

So when you have a very itchy mosquito bite or if you've been pinched, try rubbing your other arm in the same place or thinking pleasant thoughts. You might be able to trick your brain out of feeling the pain.

Biographies

Dr. Peter Adams is with the Watershed Ecosystems Programme at Trent University. He's particularly interested in the ecological importance of the ice that covers lakes in winter. Ice can block light, killing aquatic plants, with subsequent effects up the food chain. The ice cover can even alter the chemistry of lake water.

◆

Canada's first female astronaut, **Dr. Roberta Bondar**, spent eight days in orbit in January 1992. She is both a scientist and a medical doctor. Dr. Bondar is especially interested in how the brain and the eyes work together to allow us to see, and how those processes might be disrupted in the weightlessness of space.

◆

Dr. Paul Corey has spent much of his time at the University of Toronto trying to make sense of studies of workers' health. Because younger, healthier workers often have the dirtiest jobs, and less healthy workers retire from work at a younger age, it might look as though dirty jobs are good for your health. It is flaws of logic like this one that Dr. Corey works to expose.

◆

Working from the Royal Tyrrell Museum, **Dr. Philip Currie** has made many dramatic finds, including the world's earliest known bird footprints, in the Peace River Canyon in British Columbia. His most recent research suggests that dinosaurs undertook two vast migrations every year: one north to the Arctic, the other back south into more temperate latitudes.

◆

Besides creating the Ornithopter, **Dr. James DeLaurier** has designed a small aircraft that uses power from the ground. A microwave beam focused on the aircraft furnishes power for the inboard electric motor that turns the propeller. He works at the University of Toronto's Institute for Aerospace Studies.

Dr. Roger Downer at the University of Waterloo is using his knowledge of how insects regulate chemicals in their bodies and how they deal with stress, to develop new, safer and more environment-friendly insecticides.

◆

Along with Jane Goodall (who studied chimpanzees) and Dian Fossey (who studied gorillas), **Dr. Biruté Galdikas** is one of the three pre-eminent 20th-century chroniclers of the lives of the great apes. She has been living with and studying the orangutans in Borneo for 20 years and is president and founder of the Orangutan Foundation International. For four months of each year she lectures at Simon Fraser University.

◆

Dr. Michael Hawes of the Human Performance Lab at the University of Calgary has measured more than 10,000 feet on three continents. He has shown that people of different ages, activity levels and ethnic backgrounds have different shaped feet. A major sports shoe company has used his information to design new sneakers.

◆

One Halloween night, **Dr. Jim Hesser** and another astrophysicist discovered a new star called ZZ Ceti, the first of a new class of variable stars. These days Dr. Hesser, director of the Dominion Astrophysical Laboratory, studies the very old stars in globular clusters to learn what happened in space some 15 billion years ago, when these clusters were formed.

◆

The mountains called the Canadian Cordillera have been **Dr. Cathie Hickson**'s laboratory for 10 years. She is trying to understand why volcanoes occur where they do. Her findings suggest that there are deep crustal faults along the west side of the Rocky Mountains, allowing magma to leak upward, forming volcanoes.

Dr. Brian Kooyman and his colleagues at the University of Calgary have developed a refined technique that makes it possible to identify any animal whose blood is found on ancient stone tools, even those from 5,000 years ago or more. Now archeologists will know which animals were on Stone Age menus.

◆

At the University of Manitoba, **Dr. Linda Malcolmson** is evaluating new strains of wheat to see if the pasta made from them has a texture that will appeal to people. She is an assistant professor in the Department of Foods and Nutrition.

◆

For nearly 40 years, **Dr. Ronald Melzack** has been studying pain at McGill University. He's best known as the co-creator of the "gate theory" of pain, which argues that the brain doesn't just accept every pain signal sent to it — it may "close the gate" on some of those signals even before you feel them.

◆

Dr. Al Mitchell works at the Pacific Forestry Research Centre. His recent research has demonstrated that Douglas firs benefit from fertilizer by using sunlight more efficiently. This allows the trees to grow more rapidly and reach maturity sooner.

◆

The Human Neurosciences Research Unit at the University of Ottawa is where **Dr. Janet Mullington** studies sleep. Recently she's discovered that narcoleptics — people who have trouble staying awake — take naps at different times than most people.

◆

Like many other researchers, **Dr. Allan Paivio**, at the University of Western Ontario, is trying to figure out exactly how we remember and learn. For years he has been arguing that we use both images and words, and combinations of the two, in these two mental tasks.

Answers

Credits

Dr. Jacob Sivak is in the School of Optometry at the University of Waterloo. Originally an optometrist, he has devoted much of his research to understanding how animals or birds that spend part of their lives under water are able to adapt to seeing in both water and air.

◆

Science has taken Dr. Nancy Van Wagoner, a geology professor at Acadia University, all over the world. She witnessed the birth of the Mauna Ulu volcano in Hawaii, and she spent a month on an ice island in the Arctic looking for ancient undersea volcanoes. She's interested in billion-year-old volcanoes in Canada because they tell us what the Earth was like when they erupted.

◆

A professor of both chemistry and physics at Dalhousie University, Dr. Mary Anne White is known worldwide. Her research examines how heat is stored in and moves through materials with unusual arrangements of molecules.

◆

Dr. Harold (Buster) Welch, of the federal Department of Fisheries and Oceans, has spent 25 years researching the productivity of food chains in the Arctic. He's discovered that adding phosphorus and nitrogen to Arctic lakes greatly increases the rate of growth of arctic char and lake trout.

◆

A pioneer in using computer models to understand how monkeys and apes see, Dr. Steven Zucker is a professor of electrical engineering at McGill University. Now he is applying his knowledge of animal vision to the design of robot vision.

Ancient Garbage
It's a bedroom containing:
1. a sneaker
2. parts of a hamburger on a plate
3. a poster of a rock musician
4. a water bed and pillow
5. a telephone.

Tale of a Tree
1. Yes, there is a set of three very narrow summer rings in the years 1983, 1984 and 1985. With so few leaves, the tree was unable to gather sunlight to make new material for growth.

2. There's another year that seems to be just like that: 1989. A cool spring does not give the tree much chance to grow, so the springwood part of the ring, the light-colored part, is quite narrow. But the hot, wet summer is great for trees, and so the dark summerwood part of the ring is unusually wide.

3. Although the fire didn't kill the tree, it looks as though it did reach the tree and slow its growth dramatically. This year is the only one where both the springwood and summerwood parts of the ring are very narrow.

4. The head of the nail is in the sixth ring from the center, so the tree was only six years old, not ten, when the logger hammered the nail in.

Dinosaur Detective
1. One carnivorous (meat-eating) dinosaur and two herbivorous (plant-eating) dinosaurs made these footprints.

2. The dinosaur walking in from the bottom was the attacker. He started to run, taking longer steps, when he saw dinner ahead of him.

3. This herbivore turned and ran off to escape the attacker.

4. This flurry of footprints occurs where the second herbivore met his fate. The meat-eater, then with a full stomach, ambled off to the top of the page.

Permission to use the photos within *Real Live Science* was obtained through the courtesy of the following individuals and organizations:

p. 6 (top) Dr. Stephen Zucker, (bottom) McGill University; 8 Canadian Space Agency; 10 (top) Brian Noble/The Ex Terra Foundation, (bottom) Mike Todor/The Ex Terra Foundation; 12 Dr. Allan Paivio; 14 Miles Ecclestone/ Trent University; 16 Jolley-Dotson/ The Orangutan Foundation International; 18 Maurice Green/Dr. Roger Downer; 20 Dr. Paul Corey; 22 D. J. Reinisch/Dr. Linda Malcolmson; 24 (left) ©T. A. Wiewandt/ DRK Photo, (right) Dr. Alan Mitchell; 26 Dr. Harold Welch; 28 Dr. Michael Hawes; 30 Dr. Janet Mullington; 32 (top) Mary-Clare Carder/Dr. James Hesser, (bottom) The Canada-France-Hawaii Telescope Corporation; 34 (top) Lisa Stephen/Dr. Brian Kooyman, (bottom) Brian Kooyman; 36 Dr. Jacob Sivak; 38 Bruce Cohoon/Acadia University; 38-39 ©John Hyde/ Bruce Coleman Inc.; 40 Maclean's Magazine; 42 (top left) J. J. Nagel/Dr. Catherine Hickson, (top right) Dalhousie University, (bottom) © John Marshall; 44 Dr. Ronald Melzack.

Index